KRISTENA EDEN

BAPTISM PROMISES

SPECIAL COVENANTS ON MY BAPTISM DAY

PIONEER PLUS
SPRINGVILLE, UTAH

© 2015 Kristena Eden
All rights reserved

No part of this book may be reproduced in any form whatsoever, whether by graphic, visual, electronic, film, microfilm, tape recording, or any other means, without prior written permission of the publisher, except in the case of brief passages embodied in critical reviews and articles.

This is not an official publication of The Church of Jesus Christ of Latter-day Saints. The opinions and views expressed herein belong solely to the author and do not necessarily represent the opinions or views of Cedar Fort, Inc. Permission for the use of sources, graphics, and photos is also solely the responsibility of the author.

ISBN 13: 978-1-4621-1782-6

Published by Pioneer Plus, an imprint of Cedar Fort, Inc.
2373 W. 700 S., Springville, UT 84663
Distributed by Cedar Fort, Inc., www.cedarfort.com

LIBRARY OF CONGRESS CATALOGING-IN-PUBLICATION DATA

Eden, Kristena.
 Baptism promises / Kristena Eden.
   pages cm
 Includes bibliographical references.
 ISBN 978-1-4621-1782-6 (saddlestitch : alk. paper)
 1. Baptism--Church of Jesus Christ of Latter-day Saints. I. Title.
 BX8655.3.E34 2015
 264'.09332081--dc23
                                                       2015026089

Cover and page design by Lauren Error
Cover design © 2015 by Lyle Mortimer
Edited by Eileen Leavitt

Printed in the United States of America

10 9 8 7 6 5 4 3 2 1

Printed on acid-free paper

ON MY BAPTISM DAY

[Photo of you in white]

[Photo of all who helped on this day]

Getting baptized is like opening the door to our Heavenly Father and Savior, Jesus Christ. Jesus showed us what we need to do to enter Heavenly Father's door. He was baptized by immersion, which means being completely covered with water. Being buried in water reminds us of how Jesus died for us. When we come out of the baptism water, it reminds us that Jesus was resurrected and that we can also live again after we die. Heavenly Father loves us and knows our names. He wants us to come back home to Him, and baptism is the start of our journey back.

Confirmation is another important step for us to return to Heavenly Father. This ordinance is one that can help us to feel His love while we are still on this earth. Priesthood holders put their hands on our heads. They give us a blessing and a gift. The gift of the Holy Ghost will help us to remember to do what is right and keep our baptismal promises.

I PROMISE TO KEEP HIS COMMANDMENTS

In the scriptures, we read that Heavenly Father loved us, so He sent His Son, Jesus Christ, to set the example. What do we do when we really love others? We believe in them, and we try hard to help them. Jesus loved us so much that He freely gave His life for us. He did that so we can prepare to return to heaven. Jesus could have chosen not do so much to help us, yet He wanted us to be happy for eternity. In return, we can honor His choice and His love by keeping His commandments. We promise this when we are baptized.

FIND AND FOLLOW THE COMMANDMENTS

```
I F Y S A C R A M E N T R G O
U L O T H C R U H C V E N E M
E T K N E E P M Y C M I F O M
M A E E N D M E N E T T A S U
V U I M Y E P O M S Q H M Z J
K W V D P C Q B A Z S P I E L
Y G B N X L E F L C Q R L U M
M E C A W R E V R T J A Y S N
H J I M J A P I O N K Y N V E
T U D M A B P R L L M E U E Z
U E F O K T G E O R T R R A S
W D W C U V N E S T U T F Q A
K M Q R T I T H I N G A Q I K
X W E G Y N I D Y B I M Z U V
B S G F E K K J C W U J Z T S
```

FIND THE FOLLOWING WORDS:

CHURCH   LOVE   SCRIPTURES
COMMANDMENTS   PRAYER   TEMPLE
FAMILY   REMEMBER   TITHING
FASTING   SACRAMENT

I PROMISE TO CHOOSE THE RIGHT

When we are baptized, we promise Heavenly Father that we will continue to choose the right. The best part of this promise is that when we do make mistakes, we can repent. We partake of the sacrament each week to remind us of our baptismal day and to allow us to keep trying to be more like Jesus. We must be very important to our Heavenly Father for Him to give us a way to keep learning to do better. We can repent and ask Him to forgive us—that is when we can feel His love the most. The scriptures tell us, "For my yoke is easy, and my burden is light" (Matthew 11:30). When we do our best to choose the right, we can feel our burdens become light.

CHOOSING THE RIGHT

Crack the code by matching the letters given in the key to the symbols under each blank letter space.

A	B	C	D	E	F	G	H	I	J	K	L	M
N	Φ	Ξ	Λ	ς	Ψ	Z	H	χ	Π	Γ	Σ	Θ

N	O	P	Q	R	S	T	U	V	W	X	Y	Z
T	Ω	E	K	A	I	O	Δ	P	M	Υ	ζ	Ï

__ __ __ __ __
χ M χ Σ Σ

__ __ __ __ __ __ __ __ __ __ __
E A Ω Θ χ I ς O Ω Γ ς ς E

__ __ __ __ __ __ __ __ __ __
O A ζ χ T Z O Ω Λ Ω Θ ζ

__ __ __ __ __ __ __ __ __ __ __
Φ ς I O N T Λ Σ χ I O ς T

__ __ __ __ __ __ __ __ __ __ __
O Ω M H N O H ς N P ς T Σ ζ

__ __ __ __ __ __ __ __ __
Ψ N O H ς A M N T O I

__ __ __ __ __ __ .
Θ ς O Ω Λ Ω

I BECOME A MEMBER OF THE CHURCH OF JESUS CHRIST OF LATTER-DAY SAINTS

When we are baptized and confirmed, we become members of The Church of Jesus Christ of Latter-day Saints. Being a member of the Church is having another home. The power of the priesthood is upon the earth and is given to the priesthood holders to bless us. It is wonderful how much love our Savior, Jesus Christ, shows all of us. With our membership, we have the gift of the Holy Ghost, and He can penetrate deep in our hearts so that we can feel more of our Savior's love. By becoming a member, we can gain more understanding of His plan and how we fit in this home of unconditional love. The opportunity of being a member of Christ's Church is part of this great plan of happiness.

I AM A MEMBER

ACROSS

1. Our Savior
2. The second step to becoming a member*
4. The first step to becoming a member*
7. The authority of God
8. A weekly reminder of our responsibility of being a member

DOWN

1. A two-way promise we make with Heavenly Father
3. How we receive the Gift of the Holy Ghost
5. God's plan for us
6. What Heavenly Father feels toward His children

*Articles of Faith 1:4

JESUS PROMISES THAT I CAN HAVE THE HOLY GHOST WITH ME

If we live worthily, we can have the Holy Ghost to be our companion and friend to help us. He is there to guide, teach us, and comfort us. If we take time to pray and to listen, we will recognize promptings that can teach us. Sometimes, promptings come as a small voice or as an idea. It can also be a feeling of peace that what we are doing is good. When we follow these promptings, we feel comfort. The more we follow these promptings, the more often they come, and the more comfort we feel. The feelings we get from the Holy Ghost are good and happy feelings. Through the feelings of the Holy Ghost, we know that Heavenly Father is watching over us.

FRUITS OF THE SPIRIT

UNSCRAMBLE THE WORDS BELOW TO SEE WHAT BLESSINGS YOU GET FROM HAVING THE HOLY GHOST AS A COMPANION.

1. otCrmfo   _____
2. ecPea   _____
3. dinGeuca   _____
4. Chopnansmipio _____
5. yJo   _____
6. hFtia   _____
7. wensrAs   _____
8. voLe   _____
9. seHpanisp   _____

JESUS PROMISES THAT MY SINS ARE FORGIVEN

Jesus forgives us of our sins when we are baptized. *Repentance* is another name for the process of how we become perfect. This is like us changing our old path for a new one. We can change the direction of our lives to better follow Jesus and His teachings. The reason Jesus can promise us that our sins are and will be forgiven is because He paid the price for us. He atoned for our sins so that we can have the choice to repent when we make a mistake. It is important to remember that repentance is available for us not only to find forgiveness but also to help us become perfect, as our Heavenly Father is perfect. Repentance will bring happiness to us and to all the people we love.

JESUS PROMISES ME FORGIVENESS

1. Faith and _____ bring peace and happiness.

2. When we ask for _____, it is almost like being baptized again.

3. Repentance is the path to _____.

4. The _____ is a weekly renewing of covenants like those made at baptism.

5. The _____ means that Jesus paid for our sins.

6. Jesus needs us to be _____ and do the best we can.

A. Sacrament

B. Atonement

C. Forgiveness

D. Perfection

E. Repentance

F. Obedient

JESUS PROMISES THAT I WILL RETURN TO LIVE WITH HEAVENLY FATHER SOMEDAY

"Verily, verily, I say unto you, ye are little children, and ye have not as yet understood how great blessings the Father hath in his own hands and prepared for you;

"And ye cannot bear all things now; nevertheless, be of good cheer, for I will lead you along. . . .

"I will go before your face. I will be on your right hand and on your left, . . . and mine angels [shall be] round about you, to bear you up.

"The kingdom is yours and the blessings thereof are yours, and the riches of eternity are yours" (D&C 78:17–18; D&C 84:88; D&C 78:18).

I WILL RETURN TO LIVE WITH HEAVENLY FATHER

GO THROUGH THE MAZE TO FIND JESUS.

START

ANSWERS

PAGE 3

```
I F Y S A C R A M E N T R G O
U L O T H C R U H C V E N E M
E T K N E E P M Y C M I F O M
M A E E N D M E N E T T A S U
V U I M Y E P O M S Q H M Z J
K W V D P C Q B A Z S P I E L
Y G B N X L E F L C Q R L U M
M E C A W R E V R T J A Y S N
H J I M J A P I O N K Y N V E
T U D M A B P R L L M E U E Z
U E F O K T G E O R T R R A S
W D W C U V N E S T U T F Q A
K M Q R T I T H I N G A Q I K
X W E G Y N I D Y B I M Z U V
B S G F E K K J C W U J Z T S
```

PAGE 5

"I will promise to keep trying to do my best and listen to what Heavenly Father wants me to do."

PAGE 7

Across: 1. Christ 2. repentance 4. faith 7. priesthood 8. sacrament

Down: 1. covenant 3. confirmation 5. happiness 6. love

PAGE 9

Comfort, Peace, Guidance, Companionship, Joy, Faith, Answers, Love, Happiness

PAGE 11

1. E 2. C 3. D 4. A 5. B 6. F